Communication

How To Break The Code Of Small Talk While Boosting
Your Social Skills And Generating Instant Likability

*(Improving Online Communication And Professional
Relationships Through The Use Of Email In Location-
independent Work Settings)*

Werner Heiss

TABLE OF CONTENT

An Outlook On Health And Wellness 1

The Potency Of Sensory Perception: Employing Verbal Expression To Evoke Vivid Imagery In The Minds Of Your Audience 11

Please Pay Attention To And Effectively Practice Listening, Reading, And Speaking Skills. 31

Ocd Myths And Truths 48

The Role Of Intuition, Vitality, And Inter-Species Communication 59

Locating The Appropriate Ladies 110

Effective Communication Tips 144

Strategies For Mitigating Interpersonal Conflicts Within A Team 168

An Outlook On Health And Wellness

This global health crisis has directed unprecedented scrutiny towards the state of global health, revealing underlying issues within and between nations grappling with conflicting perspectives, lack of confidence, anxiety, and the specter of conflict. In addition, it elicited conspicuous instances of societal fragmentation and the leaders' failure to effectively convey information and endorse prudent health measures. The United States will develop a shared recollection of this crisis and its ramifications.

Your overall well-being is deeply interconnected with your individual state of health (including physical, mental/emotional, and spiritual aspects), the quality of your relationships, and the state of society at large. Conversely, effective communication behaviors have a direct correlation with the quality of your overall health. Certain forms of communication contribute to the enrichment of individuals' lives and promote their personal well-being, whereas alternative types of interactions yield detrimental effects. As an illustration, recent social neuroscience studies have revealed that during task performance, the presence of a loved one not only elicits positive emotions but also alleviates the activation of brain regions associated with the release of stress hormones that can be detrimental to one's overall well-being. We have made the decision to designate communication behaviors that contribute positively to overall well-being as "healthy communication," while characterizing communication that poses harm to health as "unhealthy communication."

Although the term "health" is commonly utilized and comprehended, even within the medical field, there is a lack of consensus regarding a precise definition. Take a moment to contemplate the distinctions between the terms 'illness' and 'wellness.' It is conceivable for a person to experience a state of well-being, yet possess a congested coronary artery, whereas another individual may endure severe back discomfort without any discernible indication of muscular or disc impairment. An individual harboring the coronavirus may exhibit no discernible symptoms, yet remain infectious. Who is afflicted with illness and who is in good health?

The World Health Organization provides the following definition of health: It is the state of being in optimum physical, mental, and social well-being; encompassing more than just the absence of disease or weakness; and ultimately enabling individuals to lead a life that is both socially and economically productive. This definition, widely acknowledged by the World Health Organization (WHO), posits that the attainment of a state of optimal physical, psychological, spiritual well-being, and societal harmony is indeed feasible. Health is defined as the capacity to achieve optimal performance, specifically in relation to familial and occupational responsibilities. The objective is to achieve holistic well-being, which entails the overall health and vitality of an individual, in contrast to merely the absence of physical discomfort or illness. Health promotion involves the cultivation of lifestyle practices that individuals and communities, who are in good health, can embrace to uphold and augment their overall state of well-being.

Physical Disparity as the Basis for Derision

The global community has a tendency to ridicule anything that deviates from the norm. Throughout an extensive duration that surpasses our desire for acknowledgement, clowns and dwarfs have persistently served as a source of amusement within the realm of the circus. In contemporary society, the act of demeaning individuals based on their weight is widely regarded as culturally inappropriate. Nonetheless, it remains a challenge to impose limitations on comedians who exercise their creative freedom by incorporating self-deprecating humor concerning their own weight and obesity. Certain individuals employ both discreet and blatant forms of fat-shaming as a means to intentionally degrade and humiliate others. Anything that deviates from the norm, such as elongated dental structures or a prominent nasal feature, can become a subject of ridicule by those around.

Several frequently employed subjects for amusement include:

Having poor skin

Possessing protruding teeth, prominent ears, or any similar physical attributes as such

Possessing an observable anatomical malformation or impairment

Diversity based on race or ethnicity.

Here are several elements that can be employed to ridicule a child, ultimately resulting in the child experiencing a sense of social alienation or feeling out of place. This kind of derision has the potential to undermine the self-esteem of individuals, regardless of their age, which may result in a sense of isolation and insecurity.

This form of ridicule significantly influences the susceptible psyche of the child. The child bears no responsibility for the occurrence, yet the subsequent course of action is likely to lead the child towards self-isolation.

The primary challenge inherent in such matters lies in the child's lack of agency to effect any changes and the resultant sense of powerlessness that ensues. This feeling of powerlessness and absence of self-assurance pose significant obstacles for individuals striving to develop their social skills.

Additional Factors That Could Lead to Ridicule

Bullying constitutes a criminal act, albeit one that is regrettably pervasive. Children may endure instances of bullying due to factors beyond their control, thereby lacking the means to avert or undo such occurrences.

There are several prevalent factors that contribute to individuals being subjected to bullying:

Their religion

Their ethnic background

Their sexual orientation

Being poor

Their unpopular interests

Family reputation

Distinguished given or surname

Their accent

Within the familial context, children may be subjected to ridicule or derogatory comments due to:

From parents:

Due to their underperformance compared to their siblings.

For being shy

For failing to adhere to proper procedures, they may be inclined to select...

Within the educational setting, children may be subjected to ridicule and derision for the following reasons:

As a reserved child in the classroom, one who tends to maintain a consistent state of silence

Due to their meekness and insufficient inclination to assert themselves

For displaying inadequate physical strength, excessive body weight, or a lack of coordination

The Potency Of Sensory Perception: Employing Verbal Expression To Evoke Vivid Imagery In The Minds Of Your Audience

A Comprehensive Analysis of Physical and Mental Wellness

In the realm of narrative composition, a commonly employed piece of advice is to convey information through the art of visual depiction rather than straightforward declaration. Therefore, rather than explicitly informing the reader that an individual is morally deficient, it is more effective to construct a scene wherein their actions serve as evidence of their inherent lack of moral integrity.

When engaging in narrative communication, the fundamental tenet remains unchanged.

In the preceding illustration of the monomyth within the previous chapter, the orator not only imparts to his listeners the aesthetic magnificence of the sunrise, but surpasses mere description to achieve a more profound effect. However, he allows them to arrive at that conclusion independently as a primary step.

He delineates the exquisite hues that graced his vision on that particular morning, depicting a vivid portrayal of a delightful dawn for his listeners to relish in their own imaginative faculties.

Similarly, amidst his challenging circumstances, he refrains from directly expressing his unhappiness to the audience. Conversely, he imparts specific particulars that collectively construct the portrayal of a desolate individual.

To truly establish a profound connection with your audience, adhere to this method. The greater your degree of altruism in your narrative style, the more commendable it is. Convey your first-hand experience to the audience in a literal manner.

According to empirical research, it has been found that following a brief period of passive observation, an individual's cognitive function transitions to what is known as the 'alpha' state of mind. In this state, the listener's subconscious becomes susceptible and significantly more receptive to the power of suggestion.

Their cognitive faculties pertaining to logical analysis and discernment are diminished, their level of vigilance is relaxed, and, at least initially, they acquiesce to the situation regardless of their personal preferences. It is incumbent upon you to ensure they remain in that state by providing ample passive brain stimulation.

How to do that? By employing proficient narrative techniques, undoubtedly.To be more precise, through compelling narrative techniques that engage the imaginative faculties of your audience. When individuals actively employ their imaginative faculties, they tend to exhibit a diminished propensity for critical analysis of your message, while concurrently demonstrating an increased receptiveness towards novel concepts.

While recounting your narrative, provide each member of the audience with a diverse range of sensory stimuli to contemplate. Again, share your experience. Inform them of the occurrence in which you experienced a physiological reaction resulting in the appearance of goosebumps on your skin. How your stomach dropped. The sensation of a shiver traveling along your spine.

By incorporating vivid sensory descriptions like the examples provided, you can be assured of engaging your audience on an elevated level.

A Few Tangible and Impactful Perspectives to Contemplate:

Detail the physiological responses that were elicited by the event. Examples of such reactions include a mere reflexive blinking, a sudden sensation of the stomach sinking, and the constriction of the throat. Employing this technique effectively engrosses the listener in your personal experience.

Most individuals have encountered these involuntary physiological responses at some juncture in their existences. Consequently, the minds of your audience are inherently programmed to establish associations between these elements and specific stimuli.

Describe the actions performed by your hands or other bodily appendages during the occurrence. Do not disclose your anger, but describe the clenching of your hands into fists.

Avoid expressing fear and instead convey the physical manifestations such as the trembling of your fingers. Instead of stating that a person in the story appeared impatient, provide a detailed depiction of their actions, such as vigorously tapping their foot on the ground while moving at a rapid pace of sixty miles per hour.

Engage in the utilization of the present tense when narrating your story. It is likely that you may have observed that the exemplary monomyth underwent a shift in tense, particularly as it approached its climax. This alteration is considerably more discreet in an oral exposition.

Please refrain from using the phrase "and then our boat went under." Instead, kindly narrate the sequence of events leading to the shipwreck as if you are currently witnessing it in real time.

Discuss the scenario of unexpectedly finding oneself amidst ankle-deep water, appearing seemingly out of nowhere, while maintaining a present tense narrative.

This method serves as an additional valuable technique to immerse your audience within the narrative of your story.

Chapter 1

Physical Expression

Facial expressions

Facial expressions serve as indicators of both body language and emotional expression. A person's emotional disposition and cognitive state can be precisely deduced from various cues, encompassing the subtle shifts exhibited by their eyes, eyebrows, lips, nose, and cheeks. One must also consistently consider the context in which it is taking place and the probable intention of the individual.

Happiness

An individual who exudes cheerfulness typically displays a pleasant countenance adorned with a smile and tends to direct their gaze upwards more frequently. Generally speaking, there is a notable display of increased enthusiasm evident in their body language and facial expressions.

Sadness can be recognized by the lack of a smile and a noticeable unwillingness to do so. Furthermore, individuals who experience melancholy tendencies are more inclined to manifest expressions of sadness on their countenances. Especially in comparison to an individual who is experiencing satisfaction, their facial and bodily expressions will exhibit signs of diminished energy.

Focused

When an individual's attention is concentrated, their eyebrows tend to be moderately lowered and positioned towards the center of their face. In colloquial language, this phenomenon is commonly known as "knitted brows." Furthermore, their gaze exhibits heightened concentration and their overall demeanor exudes a stronger determination to successfully fulfill the task at hand. Positive emotions are commonly associated with a heightened sense of inner stability and composure. Concentration: When an individual is focused, it indicates that they have allocated utmost importance to a specific point or area of their visual perception. Elevated cognitive functioning is concurrent with this procedure. Consequently, it is occasionally characterized as displaying cognitive focus, nonetheless, this assertion can also be more comprehensively employed to depict a state of mental determination. Consequently, an individual's facial non-verbal cues may provide insight into their level of concentration, thus revealing their thoughts. An evident instance can be observed in ordinary discourse, wherein an individual directs their primary attention towards the interlocutor, employing heightened cognitive abilities to contemplate the substance of the spoken words. When an individual engages in this behavior, it gives the impression that they are directing their attention towards comprehending the other person intellectually and visually.

Unfocused

A countenance displaying an unfocused visage often showcases raised eyebrows and eyes lacking focus. Individuals lacking focus will exhibit diminished enthusiasm towards any task they are engaging with. Appearing inattentive often correlates with emotions such as depression, ennui, and apprehension.

Confident

Assertive facial body language exhibits a heightened sense of focus, composure, and vigor. Furthermore, an individual who displays confidence is significantly more inclined to engage in upward gazes and actively establish eye contact.

Chapter 3:

Effective Strategies for Maintaining Synchrony in Communication with Others

We are all aware of the distress that can arise from being misunderstood. You express a statement, yet it assumes a completely divergent interpretation for the recipient, subsequently resulting in a sequence of discord, animosity, and confrontation.

Similar to other instances of errors and unfavorable circumstances, misunderstandings are merely manifestations of errors that arise during the process of perception. It pertains to the various cognitive shortcuts that the human brain employs when attempting to comprehend our intricate and multifaceted reality. Please be advised that you have a sole opportunity to create a favorable initial impact. If you fail to meet expectations, there will be consequences. It is commonly believed that individuals tend to exercise prudence and thoughtfulness prior to forming any evaluations. If I were to inquire whether you engage in hastiness while forming an impression about someone, it is probable that you would respond in the negative. Nevertheless, it remains true that we all tend to form hasty assessments of individuals. We are all culpable of forming immediate, spontaneous impressions.

For example, when observing an individual in tears, instead of presuming that the individual may have received distressing news or is going through a difficult day, we tend to erroneously perceive the person as inherently gloomy or dealing with depression. The primary cause for the tendency of initial impressions to form hasty judgments and misunderstandings lies in the inherent inclination of our brains to conserve energy by disregarding inconsequential matters or those that bear no relevance to our existence. In the given scenario, if all we have to rely on is the sight of an individual shedding tears, it may lead us to infer that the person possesses an innate inclination towards sadness or depression. The human brain exhibits a reluctance to expend energy on cognitive processes beyond said threshold.

The true predicament arises when an individual's conduct or deeds fail to provide us with as much insight into their character as our brain's automatic response. Although it is rare to be able to change initial misconceptions, there are numerous strategies available to address and overcome them.

To mitigate these challenges, presented herewith are a series of strategies which can greatly enhance effective communication whilst minimizing the potential for misconceptions.

Chapter Two: Interpersonal Communication and its Role in Relationships

Positive personal relationships are established upon multiple elements, with open communication being among them. In the absence of efficient and transparent communication between oneself and one's close acquaintances, interpersonal connections may readily deviate from their intended course. It is crucial that you engage in these discussions by placing significant importance on active listening and adopting a respectful tone.

In the course of this chapter, we shall examine various communication styles that are most fitting for managing interactions with your significant other, your parents, your companions, and, if applicable, your offspring. Every segment will examine the four characteristics of efficient communication and their practical relevance.

Significant Other

In the context of a healthy relationship, engaging in meaningful dialogue with your partner tends to flow effortlessly. It is highly likely that you have a strong mutual understanding, which facilitates effective communication, and you are probably adept at engaging in casual conversations without difficulty. In the context of such relationships, everyday discourse tends to be relatively uncomplicated.

But what if you happen to possess a matter of utmost significance that requires deliberation? What course of action could one take if dissatisfied with a particular aspect of one's relationship or personal life? If one were contemplating significant transformations and envisioning future aspirations, how might one engage in a discourse regarding these matters with their spouse or significant other?

Engaging in these discussions can pose greater challenges. It is imperative to ensure that your intended message is unambiguous and that your beloved comprehends your standpoint. You must ensure the preservation of emotional well-being and the comprehensive comprehension of your intended communication. This is the point where the application of effective communication skills becomes crucial.

Word Choice

Exercising caution and thoughtfulness in the selection of one's words is imperative when engaged in significant discussions with one's spouse or romantic partner. It is imperative to ensure their comprehension of your message, while concurrently safeguarding their emotional well-being and avoiding any unwarranted attribution of blame.

It is highly probable that if there is a significant matter you wish to communicate to your beloved, you have likely devoted considerable thought and deliberation to it beforehand. Devote additional time to mentally rehearsing the conversation. Consider various alternative approaches to expressing your intended message, and endeavor to envision their potential reactions. Please endeavor to continually rehearse the conversation until you reach a sufficient level of ease and confidence to engage in it.

There is no obligatory need for verbal rehearsal of a conversation in order to undertake this exercise, nor is there necessitated allocation of dedicated time for its execution. One can engage in mental rehearsals of prospective conversations while multitasking, such as attending to household chores or driving. Your attention is not directed towards the actual manner in which you will articulate your message, but rather solely on the precise content of the message itself. This task can be accomplished entirely within one's own thoughts, without the need to engage in self-conscious dialogue with a mirror.

Please Pay Attention To And Effectively Practice Listening, Reading, And Speaking Skills.

Each individual possesses a trace of intelligence during their youthful years, discernibly through their attentiveness. They possess the ability to simultaneously engage in active listening and articulate their thoughts orally. As children mature, a considerable number of them experience drowsiness and disengage from attentive behavior. Nevertheless, a minority of individuals persist in listening. Eventually, they reach an advanced age and no longer remain receptive. That is truly disheartening; let us refrain from dwelling on it.

Thornton Wilder's portrayal of Gertrude Stein:

The auditory organs do not possess an equivalent to eyelids, although they can be effectively sealed in the same manner as one would close eyelids. It is possible for both senses to be temporarily inactive simultaneously; however, it is more frequently observed for the sense of hearing to be momentarily deactivated while the sense of sight remains operational. That fact holds negligible significance if one's cognitive focus is redirected from the auditory or visual stimuli in both situations. The perceptions registered by the senses are subsequently devoid of significance, be they auditory disturbances or visual depictions.

The act of listening, much like reading, primarily engages the faculties of the mind rather than the physical senses of hearing or sight. When the cognitive faculties are not actively engaged in the act, it is appropriate to designate it as hearing rather than listening, and seeing rather than reading.

A prevalent fallacy surrounding the act of listening and reading is the belief that it involves passive absorption rather than active engagement. They consistently avoid committing this mistake in both their written and spoken communication. They are aware that the act of writing and speaking requires the allocation of energy, wholehearted focus, and the exertion involved in connecting with the intellects of others through written or vocal expression. Furthermore, they acknowledge that certain individuals exhibit a greater level of proficiency in these undertakings, and that skill improvement can be achieved by attentively adhering to artistic guidelines and consistently implementing them, thereby fostering the development of adeptness in performance.

Engaging in the act of reading requires an active intellectual effort, rather than a passive visual process, akin to the act of writing. Engaging the intellect is an indispensable aspect of the act of reading, thus passive reading, characterized by mere eye movement without such intellectual involvement, cannot truly be deemed as reading.

This type of reading can be likened to engaging in television viewing for relaxation or to occupy oneself, wherein the imagery on the screen subtly transitions before the viewer. The prevalent trend of engaging in this manner of television viewing among young individuals results in their passivity as readers, characterized by the act of flipping through the pages of a book with minimal or no emphasis on the significance of the words or the overall organization and progression of the content within the book.

Allow me to employ an alternative analogy that I have previously utilized. The individual positioned as the catcher in proximity to the home plate is an individual engaged in the pursuit of baseball, akin to the pitcher located on the elevated mound. In the realm of football, this holds true for both the recipient of the forward pass and the giver of the pass in question. In either scenario, acquiring possession of the ball requires a deliberate act of extension to complete the play. Catching requires a similar level of aptitude as throwing, albeit necessitating a distinct set of skills. The game's completion necessitates the collaborative endeavorsof both players, possessing a deep synchronization with one another.

It can be likened to the process of verbal communication. The occurrence only transpires when the intellect of the reader or listener actively engages with the writer or speaker's perspectives and endeavors to comprehend them. This information has been conveyed to the recipient via written or oral communication. Engaging in the fundamental acts of reading or listening involves more than passively perceiving words through our eyes or ears. It necessitates employing our cognitive faculties to deeply penetrate and comprehend the thoughts imparted by the author or speaker. As a result, there is a disruption in communication, a total absence, and a squandering of time.

Certainly, it would be unfair to place the onus solely on the reader or listener. The catcher cannot be held accountable for failing to successfully catch a wild pitch.

Likewise, specific literary compositions and oral expressions can exhibit an absence of significance and logical structure, or they may be so convoluted and bewildering in their language usage that even the most astute reader and listener cannot decipher their intended message. Certain expressions are of such poor quality, failing to accurately convey the intended message, that they deserve very little, if any, consideration.

When contemplating the level of effort and expertise needed for attentive and proficient listening, I will assume that the verbal communication merits careful consideration and warrants the utilization of all available effort and skill in comprehending it to a level that aligns with the speaker's intended understanding.

5

FILM CLIPS

Essential components required for the execution of this dynamic include a visual medium in the form of film, and the requisite resources to facilitate its production. Posters with images

The required group size ranges from a minimum of 20 individuals to a maximum of 25 individuals.

Duration: approximately 30 to 45 minutes

The utilization of concise film excerpts assists children and adolescents diagnosed with Asperger's syndrome in recognizing and enhancing their emotional handling abilities.

Prior to commencing, a comprehensive exposition is presented delineating the nature of emotions, the techniques employed to discern them, and pertinent attributes associated therein. The assembled members are informed that in preparation for the subsequent gathering, they are required to view the designated film (at which juncture the title shall be disclosed).

While observing the aforementioned activity, their duty entails the diligent note-taking of aspects intricately connected to the realm of emotions.

After assembling, the individuals comprising the group are arranged in a circular formation, occupying adjacent seats. Subsequently, they are distributed cards or posters depicting facial expressions denoting various emotions such as happiness, sorrow, unease, apprehension, trepidation, displeasure, and so forth. The cards are distributed sequentially, with each card being handed from person to person.

Following that, an opportunity arises to engage in discourse pertaining to the film, specifically addressing the attributes they have noted as well as their connection to the posters and images.

The child or adolescent diagnosed with Asperger's syndrome is requested to allocate a visual representation to the observations they made and establish connections to the various emotional states depicted.

Once the intended goal has been attained, the individual will acquire the ability to discern their own emotional states and comprehend the presence of sadness, happiness, fear, anxiety, anger, stress, and other related emotions.

In conclusion, it is imperative to acknowledge that emotions are inherent in every individual, and that they possess neither inherent negativity nor harm, provided that we acquire the skills to effectively regulate and channel them.

Facilitators offer suitable tools and exercises to facilitate the accomplishment of this objective, while also creating an environment where participants are encouraged to openly articulate their emotions and insights gained throughout the progression of the activities.

CHAPTER FIVE

KEY 3

NON-VERBAL COMMUNICATION SKILLS

Efficient communication entails the utilization of both spoken and nonverbal signals. By enhancing your understanding of your bodily movements and vocal expressions, you can improve your capacity to effectively convey messages and make presentations.

Examining and valuing non-verbal communication.

Nonverbal communication comprises the predominant portion of every message. Based on various predictions, this could conceivably encompass a substantial majority, reaching as high as 80%, of overall communication. It is of utmost importance to actively take into account and fully grasp non-verbal communication, particularly in situations where it is lacking or reduced, such as during written correspondence or telephonic conversations.

Non-verbal communication is often misinterpreted as solely pertaining to body language, despite its broader scope. It encompasses, yet extends beyond, vocal intonation and frequency, physical gestures, visual engagement, body stance, and facial countenance, in addition to physiological manifestations such as perspiration.

Consequently, by diligently observing the non-verbal signals of individuals, one can acquire a more profound comprehension of their thoughts and emotions. Moreover, it is important to uphold consistency in both your verbal communication and nonverbal cues to enhance the effectiveness of your message.

CHAPTER SEVEN

ADDITIONAL ELEMENTS THAT MAY IMPACT COMMUNICATION

Moreover, a plethora of supplementary factors and variables can exert an influence on the transmission and reception of a message. These encompass your utilization of wit, your overall demeanor towards individuals, and your personal outlook—both regarding life as a whole and towards the individual and communication.

Utilizing Humour

The act of laughing triggers the release of endorphins, which have demonstrated the ability to mitigate feelings of tension and anxiety. The majority of individuals derive pleasure from laughter and are naturally drawn to individuals who possess the ability to elicit laughter from them. Do not hesitate to exhibit wit or intelligence, however, ensure that your humor is contextually suitable. Employ your intelligence to establish rapport, dismantle barriers, and garner the goodwill of peers. By utilizing suitable wit and levity, you will enhance your perceived charm.

Treat Individuals Equally

Endeavor to engage in communication with others on a level playing field, refraining from condescending or patronizing behavior. Refrain from engaging in gossip or displaying favoritism, and instead strive to treat all individuals with equanimity and parity, thereby cultivating an atmosphere of trust and reverence. If maintaining confidentiality is a matter of concern, it is crucial to ensure that its parameters are clearly comprehended and upheld.

Exert Endeavors to Address Disputes

It is nearly always advantageous to address arguments and conflicts promptly, rather than allowing them to persist. Proficient negotiators are also skilled at mediating and facilitating communication. They exhibit impartiality and fairness, actively promoting the resolution of conflicts instead of harboring prejudice or passing judgment.

Maintain an optimistic demeanor and wear a cheerful expression

Not many individuals derive pleasure from the presence of an individual burdened with unhappiness. Strive to exhibit amicability, joviality, and a positive outlook when interacting with others. Sustain a constructive and amiable disposition towards life: uphold optimism and derive insights from your failures when circumstances diverge from expectations. Individuals are inclined to exhibit a favorable response towards you if you consistently display a pleasant countenance and sustain a state of cheerfulness.

Likewise, in the event that something incites rage or agitation within you, it is advisable to allocate a few hours for the purpose of regaining composure prior to engaging in any action. If it is necessary for you to register a complaint, kindly do so in a measured manner, while considering the aspects of the situation that may be favorable and refraining from undue criticism.

Reduce Stress

Inherent stress is a characteristic of specific communication environments. However, stress can pose a significant obstacle to effective communication. Henceforth, it is imperative that all parties make a concerted effort to uphold their poise and concentration.

OcdMythsAnd Truths

Despite the prevalence often attributed to OCD, a substantial majority lacks a comprehensive grasp of its true implications. Influenced by the perceptions portrayed through social media or cinematic representations, they fabricate notions about the affliction within their minds. When queried about whether OCD constitutes a mental disorder, a possible response could be that it is purely a matter of personal disposition or ingrained behavior patterns. Many individuals tend to oversimplify and categorize all cases of OCD as a mere inclination towards tidiness and organization, lacking a comprehensive understanding of the condition. Although not entirely inaccurate, it fails to adequately depict the disarray and profound significance it holds within our society. The inclination towards maintaining orderly arrangements may be seen as commonplace, however, Obsessive-Compulsive Disorder (OCD) relinquishes this inclination of being merely a desire. On the contrary, individuals afflicted with OCD perceive the act of maintaining order as an imperative component of their daily existence. It is imperative to address the compulsion for order and equilibrium. It is an undeniable obligation. An individual who has been diagnosed with Obsessive-Compulsive Disorder (OCD) may experience difficulties in performing optimally due to the persistent occurrence of intrusive thoughts. They contemplate whether they have inadvertently left the gas on, the reason behind the misalignment of the neck of the interlocutor's T-shirt, and seek guidance on resolving the issue without appearing peculiar. These thoughts do not dissipate as readily as they entered. They become immobilized and subsequently experience growth, manifesting a strong urge to rectify the issue and provide solace. Herein lie several misapprehensions and fallacious convictions surrounding OCD.

- Germaphobes:

A regrettable falsehood propagated by the media to their extensive and uninformed viewership is the misconception that individuals with OCD are characterized by excessive hand washing and a fear of germs. Although this statement holds some truth, it merely skims the surface of the true depth and complexity of OCD. In order to alleviate the anxiety triggered by concerns of acquiring an infection or being exposed to germs, individuals incessantly engage in the act of washing whenever they encounter a surface that their mind deems as unsanitary or contaminated. This behavior persists despite their inability to eliminate these obsessive thoughts from their consciousness. However, it should be noted that this does not encompass the entirety of OCD symptoms, contrary to the portrayal often depicted in cartoons, comedies, and Facebook posts. Although germaphobia is a serious manifestation of OCD and should not be trivialized, there are alternative manners in which

OCD impacts individuals, and they carry equal severity. Individuals diagnosed with obsessive-compulsive disorder (OCD) may experience an urge to repeatedly engage in certain actions in order to alleviate their anxiety and restore a sense of balance. As previously mentioned, there are individuals who experience social discomfort related to maintaining direct eye contact or fear of perceiving objects in their peripheral vision. To certain individuals, it represents a struggle against intrusive ideations, specifically concerns regarding potentially deviant sexual inclinations. In essence, it should be noted that germaphobia is not the sole manifestation of obsessive-compulsive disorder, and it is important to recognize that not all individuals diagnosed with OCD display germaphobic tendencies.

CHAPTER 5: Eleven invaluable personal strategies for cultivating assertiveness

The ability to make assertions is an acquirable skill, so there is no need for concern if you have not yet mastered it. I may have been similar to yourself—someone whose preferred style of communication leaned towards passivity rather than assertiveness. During conversations, there is a possibility of being interrupted by someone in the group, which prompts me to adopt a nonchalant attitude, acknowledging that it does not hold significant importance. I sought to avoid inconveniencing others, and to be candid, I harbored a sense of apprehension. I was uncertain about where to commence as my confidence and proficiency in effectively conveying my thoughts were dubious to me.

When recounting this narrative, individuals anticipate a pivotal moment, an occurrence that would indeed enhance its vibrancy, albeit at the expense of veracity. In reality, I simply desired a shift in circumstances. I aspired to improve myself, achieve greater success, and serve as a role model for others. I desired the ability to assert myself in order to ensure that my perspective would be duly acknowledged, rather than being disregarded at will.

Listed below are the valuable recommendations that have greatly assisted me in improving my communication skills to ensure they are both healthier and more efficient:

Assess your manner of communication

I firmly advocate the notion that one should consistently commence with personal introspection; hence, chapter one is wholly dedicated to the exploration of various communication styles. Have you already determined or established your answer?

Do you refrain from speaking when the opportunity presents itself? Do you accept additional tasks even when your workload capacity is already reached? It appears that you are inclined towards a passive communication style.

Do you possess a tendency to hastily pass judgments or assign blame? Do individuals exhibit apprehension or trepidation when engaging in conversation with you? If that is indeed the case, then it is possible that you exhibit tendencies towards an assertive mode of communication.

If you remain uncertain, you may consider consulting with your acquaintances and relatives. Upon inquiring, they forthrightly revealed my preferred mode of communication. Furthermore, I have found it to be quite valuable to gain insight into your preferred method of communication by carefully observing and monitoring your behavior.

For instance, consider the upcoming opportunity to chronicle instances when a verbal response could have been offered but was ultimately withheld. This aligns with the passive style of communication. In contrast, one could observe the instance wherein an excessive emotional response occurred upon receiving an unfavorable remark regarding one's newly acquired skirt from a friend. Now you are aware that you are inclining towards adopting an assertive approach. Gain a thorough comprehension of your communication style prior to embarking on any modifications.

Interpersonal Conflict

When a disagreement arises between two or more team members, it gives rise to an interpersonal conflict. Such an occurrence is an inevitable result that arises when individuals possessing varying personalities and beliefs are required to collaborate closely within a confined space, all whilst pursuing a common objective. This contention can encompass a spectrum of dimensions, encompassing both emotional and physical aspects, as well as professional components, all of which may intertwine elements pertaining to both your personal life and your professional endeavors.

This conflict need not necessarily be regarded as negative, as it can potentially facilitate the discovery of shared perspectives amongst team members in unanticipated manners. Additionally, it can foster a climate that motivates individuals to devise remedies to previously encountered obstacles, fostering a synergy that would otherwise have been overlooked by the team.

There exists a total of six distinct classifications of interpersonal conflict:

Pseudo conflict typically occurs within close interpersonal relationships, such as a marital union or among siblings, and encompasses elements of playful teasing and taunting.

Factual disagreement—when there is a discrepancy among team members regarding the veracity of the information

Value discord—encompasses the divergent convictions held by distinct individuals and their awareness regarding the values espoused by others.

policy discord—when the validity or effectiveness of a proposed course of action or policy is contested, resulting in strained relations among individuals

Conflict driven by egotism—where all parties are primarily focused on prevailing in the argument, with the ego being a significant factor, consequently making the attainment of resolution more arduous.

Meta-discord arises from the divergence of opinions among the members regarding the communication methodology employed.

Interpersonal Conflict Demonstrated

It is crucial to be vigilant in observing your team for indications of conflict, and the subsequent are a few illustrations of what to be mindful of:

The prevailing conflict often arises from the deliberation surrounding remuneration, particularly when a team member asserts their entitlement to an augmentation, while their supervisor holds a divergent viewpoint.

A team necessitating cooperation for a project in which the members exhibit discord regarding the preferred course it should undertake, with a lack of willingness from any individual to make concessions.

The unjust promotion of a team member will undoubtedly result in the emergence of conflicts.

It is essential to bear in mind that a collective of individuals entails a plethora of distinct personalities, which will inevitably lead to disagreements and conflicts. When the redirection of this conflict is channeled into a creative outlet, your team can accomplish significant achievements.

The Role Of Intuition, Vitality, And Inter-Species Communication

The Role of Intuition in Animal Communication

What is intuition? Intuition can be understood as an innate faculty that enables us to access and interpret the wealth of information present in our surroundings by means of our inherent sensory mechanisms. It manifests as the intuition residing within our visceral instincts, or the intellectual synthesis we achieve by merging disparate concepts into a coherent and novel framework. Intuition circumvents the rational faculty and is ingrained within the human psyche.

Based on the perspective of contemporary physicists, the fundamental nature of all entities is energy. We represent manifestations of energy coexisting within an encompassing energy field. Information can be stored within energy, which can be perceived by our intuitive faculties. Our innate perception has the ability to access more nuanced cues than our sensory faculties alone. Due to our preoccupation with our physical encounters, we frequently fail to recognize the subtle intuitive messages we receive on a daily basis. Given that animal communication relies on intuition as its primary form of communication, enhancing your intuitive capacities directly corresponds to enhancing your aptitude for animal communication.

Human beings possess a five-dimensional nature.

Could you kindly enlighten me on the five dimensions? The five dimensions encompass the corporeal, cognitive, affective, transcendental, and dynamic facets of our individual existence. Every dimension presents to us a distinct opportunity to perceive and navigate our existence. The five dimensions can be encountered in isolation, however, they are intricately intertwined, culminating in a sophisticated system of reciprocal influences. By means of our chakras and energy meridians, the energetic realm governs the remaining four levels. This renders our dynamic self as the guardian of our entire being.

Comprehending the concept of energy is paramount to gaining insight into intuition, which consequently serves as the foundation for developing proficiency in animal communication. Hence, the initial task that I assign to my aspiring animal communicators in the Animal Communicator Academy is to cultivate their acquaintance with their energy fields.

Social Pragmatics

SCD is commonly known as Social Pragmatic Communication Disorder (SPCD). This is due to a lack of comprehension of social pragmatics among individuals with SCD.

Social pragmatics pertains to the manner in which individuals employ language in the context of social interactions. Pragmatics pertain to the unspoken conventions that dictate interpersonal communication. This encompasses both the content and the manner in which individuals express themselves. Social pragmatics encompass the strategies we employ in our daily interactions. These conventions serve as the unspoken norms that we rely upon in our daily interactions for effective communication. These actions encompass behaviors such as initiating greetings, sustaining eye contact, respecting conversational turn-taking, and adhering to the subject at hand. Though these regulations may appear self-evident to the majority, their clarity might not be apparent to individuals afflicted with SCD.

Individuals affected by sickle cell disease face challenges when it comes to discerning the distinction between the literal and figurative aspects of language. They interpret everything literally and experience confusion when presented with figurative language. As an illustration, in the event that an individual were to express, "I am famished to the point that I could consume an entire dwelling!", a child diagnosed with Sickle Cell Disease (SCD) would experience perplexity concerning the intention behind such an unusual desire to ingest a house.

In addition, non-verbal communication encompasses elements such as interpersonal gaze, facial demeanor, and bodily gestures. Frequently, they exhibit a tendency to avoid direct eye contact during interpersonal conversations and experience difficulty interpreting and understanding nonverbal cues, such as facial expressions and body language.

Furthermore, within the realm of pragmatics, consideration is also given to the suitability of exchanges in relation to a particular context. They encounter difficulty in effectively adapting their language to suit various audiences. Typically, individuals tend to employ a distinct manner of communication when engaging with a young child compared to conversing with close acquaintances or individuals of higher position. Individuals with sickle cell disease communicate with all individuals in an equitable manner. Consequently, this implies that their interactions with teachers mimic their casual conversations with friends, thereby frequently resulting in disciplinary issues within the school setting.

Additionally, they possess a propensity to engage in prolonged discourse on matters that capture their interest, promptly diverting the trajectory of the conversation whenever it veers away from their areas of interest. Frequently, they exert control over the conversation, delving into topics that the other party is already familiar with or commencing a story midway, omitting relevant details.

Children afflicted with sickle cell disease encounter challenges related to:

•The appropriate protocol for acknowledging individuals in various contexts

•Disseminating pertinent information in accordance with the context

• Adaptation of speech to suit specific contexts

• Exercising moderation in their speech volume •Regulating their vocal intensity during communication • Employing restraint in their verbal projection • Maintaining a measured tone when speaking

• Adopting distinct communication styles when conversing with children compared to interacting with teachers and other adults.

- Engaging in reciprocal dialogue exchanges

- Engaging in the habit of expressing peculiar or unrelated statements

- Comprehending and deciphering the vocal inflections utilized by individuals

- Reading facial expressions

- Deciphering social signals by observing the non-verbal cues displayed by others.

- Discerning figures of speech such as idioms, wit, metaphors, and sarcasm

- Subjects/assignments that fail to capture their interest.

- Acknowledging and honoring the physical boundaries of others

- Displaying a receptive attitude towards constructive feedback • Demonstrating a capacity for handling criticism with tact and poise • Exhibiting an awareness and openness to constructive critique

- Gaining insight into alternative perspectives

- Repeating content

- Cultivating and maintaining social relationships

Chapter 5: Maintain your concentration, devise a strategy, and adhere to it

In contemporary times, it is a frequently observed occurrence to witness individuals delivering lackluster presentations within the realms of the corporate arena, a practice which can be deemed synonymous with inflicting psychological distress. Furthermore, it is considered disadvantageous if your content fails to captivate and retain the enduring interest of your audience, irrespective of the intrinsic value it holds.

Here we present a compilation of pragmatic strategies for maintaining concentration and delivering captivating presentations that will effectively captivate your audience, thereby ensuring their sustained attentiveness to your message:

Remain focused on the subject matter

It is imperative that you ensure your audience is cognizant of your objective within the initial two minutes of your meeting. Ensure that they comprehend the significance of the information you are presenting and the benefits it will bestow upon them. During the duration of these two minutes, it is imperative that you articulate your proposed itinerary. Adhere to it, and thus, individuals can collectively remain concentrated in anticipation of a productive and enlightening presentation session.

Adhere to the designated timeframe

The era of lengthy two-hour meetings and presentations has come to an end. It is unreasonable to anticipate individuals to maintain their concentration solely while seated at a personal computer for an extended period of time. You shouldn't spend more time than expected at your session. If it is feasible, please endeavor to render it more concise. It is preferable to conduct a presentation session of shorter duration, focusing on concise and straightforward points, as this approach tends to yield greater productivity. If the content exceeds an optimal length, individuals may disengage and become susceptible to distractions posed by coworkers, electronic communications, and online advertisements.

Exhibit Awareness towards the 10-Minute Rule

Many speakers often overlook the fact that audience engagement tends to diminish after approximately 10 minutes. They persist in an uninterrupted discourse for prolonged durations, transitioning from one monotonous visual presentation to another, oblivious to the impact it is having on the spectators.

When formulating your presentation, it is advisable to establish a strategic approach to elicit periodic audience engagement within intervals of approximately 10 minutes. Posing a well-crafted inquiry, narrating a concise anecdote, presenting a succinct audio-visual presentation, or prompting the audience to scrutinize an illustrative graph are approaches capable of instigating the desired shift in the ambiance.

Show courtesy towards the audience.

Redirecting the focus from oneself towards the audience is the optimal approach for engaging and invigorating the spectators. A declaration such as, "There is an abundance of exceptional talent present in this room." I encourage you to actively engage in sharing your thoughts and opinions on the subject matter, thereby fostering a collaborative environment where mutual learning can take place.

Establish Interconnections for Individuals

When delivering a presentation, assist individuals in perceiving the seamless transition between your slides, enabling them to discern your progress and anticipate the intended trajectory. Utilize transitional phrases such as "To begin with," "Furthermore," "Moreover," "Notably," and "Significantly." These linguistic devices facilitate the audience's comprehension of the underlying significance, prompting them to pose thought-provoking inquiries such as: "What is the rationale behind this?" "What are the implications?" and "What advantages can be derived from this?" Individuals who have become disengaged will experience a revival of interest and re-involvement in the presentation.

Acquire the Skill of Utilizing Inquiries

Open-ended inquiries hold significant merit within presentations, although posing them spontaneously poses a considerable challenge. While making your preparations, compile a selection of these questions that can be accessed and utilized as needed. These inquiries and remarks serve a valuable purpose in sustaining the dialogue. Instances of these inquiries include: "In what manner would you elucidate it?," "Are you capable of envisioning yourself being present?," "Might you kindly provide additional information?," "How would you draw a conclusion?," and "By what means did we arrive at this point?"

Chapter Two: The Integration of Introverts in Professional Environments

Distinguishing between employees who possess introverted and extroverted traits does not necessitate significant effort; a mere observation is sufficient for this purpose. Participating in dialogues with different colleagues and coworkers will provide you with a comprehensive understanding of individuals who possess introverted or extroverted qualities. Managers frequently employ this knowledge to categorize their employees and allocate them tasks that align with their individual dispositions.

Outlined below are several domains commonly employed as evaluation methodologies:

In the course of meetings, extroverted individuals tend to make significantly greater contributions in contrast to their introverted counterparts. They will express their thoughts and ideas freely, positioning themselves at the forefront of a productive brainstorming session.

Conversely, introverts would exhibit hesitance and prefer to carefully observe the entire situation, attributed to a blend of diminished self-assurance and the necessity for ample information processing time. In situations where prompt action is required from the manager, introverted individuals frequently demonstrate difficulty in promptly responding and may consequently provide inaccurate recommendations, or even become unresponsive.

Collaboration and thinking outside the box are traits that extroverts typically exhibit, contrasting with introverts who tend to have a preference for performing defined tasks as assigned. In addition, introverts rarely seek help. Furthermore, owing to the intricacy and rapidity inherent within the contemporary professional setting, introverted individuals typically find themselves falling behind their colleagues. Even when they endeavor to assimilate into the novel system, they invariably fail to keep up with the overall velocity it demands.

Multitasking - extroverted individuals exhibit a preference for engaging in simultaneous execution of various projects, whereas introverted individuals may experience their focus being fragmented when confronted with numerous tasks. Consequently, introverted personnel are frequently designated extended tasks that necessitate minimal alterations. This effectively removes them from the mainstream and relegates them to a behind-the-scenes role, thereby affording extroverts an opportunity to excel and secure top positions within an organization.

In a professional setting, introverted individuals typically encounter difficulties in workspaces that contain excessive distractions, such as open cubicles, whereas extroverted individuals heavily rely on social interactions. Additionally, on numerous occasions, individuals who are introverted may find themselves lacking considerable influence over their work assignments, subsequently diminishing their productivity. This places him at a disadvantage compared to his peers, consequently impeding his progress in terms of acquiring clients, meeting established project deadlines, or potentially advancing in his career.

Recognition - extroverts experience a sense of elation and satisfaction when their efforts are acknowledged and valued in a public forum, while introverts may experience discomfort once the focus is directed towards them.

To summarize, it can be observed that introverts possess the competence to effectively fulfill their professional responsibilities, yet they encounter challenges in garnering recognition for their achievements, often leading to their stagnation within the organizational hierarchy.

Choose a Package Concept

Which of the two, the chicken or the egg, was in existence first? A complex inquiry, akin to the contemplation of whether packages drive copy or if copy drives packages. In my viewpoint, there appears to be inadequate allocation of time towards package considerations when a robust package concept is essential for achieving a successful mailing outcome. This is precisely why numerous direct mail initiatives frequently succumb to the ailment of uniformity. Creatively novel concepts, initiatives, programs, and strategies endure the consequences of an indifferent marketing approach. The package containing the #10 white window, with its uninteresting teaser headline, fails to adequately showcase numerous genuinely exhilarating ministry programs.

Your direct mail campaign presents a valuable opportunity to engage and retain the interest of donors, a vital aspect in any relationship, necessitating the incorporation of diversity. Furthermore, the selection of the cause concept holds significant influence over the nature of the promotional strategy devised to endorse it. Certain concepts, especially those that are novel or intricate, necessitate extensive elucidation, depiction, contextual information, or distinct supplementary elements or interactive elements. All of these factors influence the manner in which the letter copy should be composed. Diverse audiences necessitate a varied packaging approach, as high-level donors, club members, and lapsed donors frequently demand a distinct and tailored approach.

A fundamental inquiry that appeals to individuals in creative roles: What constitutes conventional direct mail for your ministry? If normalcy can be recognized by you, it can also be recognized by your benefactor.

Write the Reply Device

No, the task at hand is not to simply 'write the letter.' What is the rationale behind professional copywriters prioritizing the writing of the reply device copy? I'll tell you...

The turnaround document, also known as the TAD, elucidates the underlying notion and the proposal being presented to the benefactor. It encapsulates the proposition you are putting forth while emphasizing the primary advantage of the donor's philanthropic choice. Additionally, the TAD offers precise recommendations for donation recipients to contemplate, which are referred to as "gift options."

Crafting the TAD as the initial step in the process directs the attention towards the core message of the letter, while also aiding in the evaluation of the strength and effectiveness of the case, even before the actual drafting of the letter takes place. A thoroughly crafted TAD ought to possess sufficient clarity and persuasiveness, enabling it to function independently as an effective means of soliciting funds.

Write the Letter...

For many years, enthusiasts of direct mail have been engrossed in the sophisticated practice of copywriting, which encompasses both artistic and scientific elements. And greatly vexed the grammarians among the audience. You see, a direct mail letter is designed to establish a sense of personal connection, essentially deviating from the conventional formality of a business letter. Consequently, it can be inferred that the fundamental principle for copywriters is to employ conversational language in their writing. Short sentences. Stops and starts. Incomplete sentences.Short paragraphs.Excessive utilization of the term "YOU." Incorporation of punctuation marks to mirror the rhythm and flow of a conversation. The utilization of diverse margins to emphasize significant paragraphs, and the application of underlines to draw attention to crucial sentences. Furthermore, the utilization of conjunctions such as "however," "in addition," or "it is evident that..."

The format of effective direct mail holds equal significance to the content it carries. Therefore, it is imperative not to delegate the responsibility of donor communications to secretaries or executive assistants. They possess an earnest desire to achieve perfection in all aspects: justified text, left alignment, well-crafted paragraphs, and impeccable grammar. Beautiful business letters. However, it is imperative to grasp the fact that our communication is not directed towards businesses. We are engaging in correspondence with acquaintances and collaborators.

In my past experience, I had the privilege to work under the leadership of a globally renowned ministry figure. During that time, each direct mail correspondence was subject to thorough scrutiny by an experienced executive assistant, a former English educator with an exceptional command of grammar. Mrs. The emerald-hued ballpoint pen possessed by G was revered with utmost trepidation by all individuals who composed any form of written content for her superior. After multiple attempts and persistent appeals to the president, unbeknownst to his assistant, we ultimately reached a mutually acceptable agreement that involved Mrs." The mark-ups made by G on the copy submitted for approval would be carefully reviewed and honored ... Furthermore, the approach was modified as necessary in order to effectively engage with contributors.

Here are the strategies you should possess in order to effectively navigate workplace conversations:

- Cultivate a genuine inclination towards inquisitiveness about your environment and the individuals with whom you engage in conversation. This will enhance your ability to inquire more profoundly and thoughtfully, thereby enhancing the efficacy of a conversational session.

- Engage in proactive solicitation of feedback from your colleagues regarding the efficacy of your communication abilities and areas they deem necessary for refinement. Refine your techniques for engaging in casual conversations and conversational proficiency by actively engaging with your colleagues. Seek their feedback on your performance in these interactions.

- Project self-assurance by maintaining an upright posture, exhibiting a pleasant countenance, emanating an inviting demeanor, and expressing thoughts articulately.Endeavor to cultivate a sense of assurance and mastery in one's ability to articulate and express oneself.

- Employing the appropriate vocal demeanor in professional settings carries equal weight to the content expressed. Strive to strike a delicate equilibrium between upholding a sense of professionalism while remaining amiable and approachable concurrently.

- It is imperative to maintain honesty and transparency in all workplace discussions. Concealing information or failing to be transparent regarding a matter will solely result in your colleagues and clients harboring resentment and losing faith in you.

- Exercise patience and avoid hurriedly delivering your sentences, even when faced with time constraints. A discourse gains deeper significance when the transmission and comprehension of a message occur with clarity. This objective cannot be attained through the act of making the other individual feel uneasy and hurried during conversational interactions.

- It is important to maintain emotional composure and avoid being controlled by your emotions while engaging in conversations, both in professional settings and in daily life. Take a momentary pause and consciously suppress your instinctive urge to immediately reply, so as to prevent any possibility of uttering words that may be incorrect or inappropriate.

- Disregard your prior manifestations of anxiety; they are incompatible with the pursuit of becoming an accomplished conversationalist.

Business

Engaging in casual conversation proves beneficial for fostering business relationships. It is widely acknowledged that fostering strong relationships with clients greatly benefits business enterprises. The attainment of success may be guaranteed through the mastery of both the skill of engaging in small talk and the delivery of high-quality service or products. It is imperative to ensure that all employees within your company possess proficiency in the domain of casual conversation. It is imperative for employees to actively initiate conversations with clients in order to cultivate a comfortable atmosphere for each client prior to the provision of the services offered by your company.

During a corporate gathering, it affords individuals the opportunity to assess and ascertain one another's standing and level of proficiency. In situations where a preexisting rapport exists between the individuals involved, engaging in small talk can serve as a gentle introduction prior to delving into more pragmatic subjects. It enables individuals to convey their respective ambiance and perceive the ambiance of the other party.

In a professional setting, casual conversations tend to take place primarily among colleagues who possess similar expertise. Nonetheless, it can serve as an effective strategy for bosses to cultivate a professional rapport with their subordinate staff members. An employer who requests their employees to work beyond regular hours may seek to motivate them by engaging in casual conversation, momentarily diminishing the hierarchical divide. The equilibrium between substantive discourse and casual chatter in professional settings is contingent upon the specific circumstances and is additionally swayed by the comparative power dynamic of the individuals engaged in conversation. The individual holding a higher position frequently takes charge of the conversation, as they possess the power to conclude informal discourse.

An alternative approach to fostering workplace rapport is by employing the use of personal names. Commence the conversation by addressing the individual by their name, as it aids in both remembering their name and conveying that you are specifically addressing them. It enhances the likelihood of engaging in a conversation with individuals and piques their interest, particularly in regards to how you came to possess knowledge of their name. It is advisable to refrain from employing euphemisms or alternative appellations to deceive, as such actions may elicit strong aversion from certain individuals. In cases of forgotten names, it is considered more courteous to inquire about the individual's name.

The most exemplary demonstration of fostering a robust rapport with one's clientele is. If you manage to establish a strong rapport with your client and cultivate a relationship built on trust, they will remain loyal to you irrespective of the attractive offers and stiff competition presented by your rivals. They will nonetheless proceed to purchase or avail themselves of your services.

Engaging in casual conversation proves to be an economical yet highly beneficial method for promoting your business. Engaging in light conversation is essential for establishing and enhancing professional connections. Initiate and conclude your business conversation with casual conversation to enhance the rapport. Investors place great value on financial planners, not only for their financial expertise, but also for their capacity to provide a sense of security and peace of mind.

Stay informed about current advancements

Current advancements serve as exceptional conversation starters. It would be wise to avoid discussing politically charged events in case you and the unfamiliar person hold conflicting opinions. Take into account topics such as a local community event, or inquire about a recent literary publication or a recently debuted movie. Please be advised that a model has been provided: Have you been made aware of the upcoming annual Occasion Celebration commencing in one week? I typically derive pleasure from leisurely strolling and admiring the adornments.

Offer assistance

If you encounter an individual who is struggling with a task, offering assistance is a commendable approach to initiate a conversation. Depending on the location and context of the situation, you may consider using a more formal phrasing such as this: May I have the opportunity to transport that container on your behalf? I am assuming that you are unfamiliar with the structure in question.

Kindly impart an intriguing fact

This approach is most effectively employed when encountering a situation where your captivating reality directly corresponds. When aptly applied, this approach can be highly effective in engaging another individual in conversation. Here is an example: Were you aware, to some extent, of the demonstrable fact that elevators are the safest means of transportation?

Request their viewpoint

Consider soliciting the perspective of an external party to initiate a discourse. This is an exceptional approach, particularly if you are in a different location or currently seeking pens in your company's inventory storage area. This serves as a demonstration of the means to employ this.

procedure: Among these highlighters, which one is your preferred choice? I usually employ these yellow ones, but the wax ones appear quite intriguing!

Request lunch counsel

A feasible approach to initiate a conversation with an unfamiliar individual involves inquiring about their preferred dining establishment. This can be particularly advantageous in situations such as being in an elevator or waiting for a taxi or public transportation, as it allows for efficient communication. For instance, you may inquire about preferred dining options in the vicinity. I frequently conduct business from the office located on Fifth Road, hence my curiosity about this area. The local residents, particularly those with distinctive tastes, are likely to share recommendations of their preferred dining establishments. It is possible that they may extend an invitation for you to join them for lunch.

CHAPTER TWO

What is your method for initiating interactions with unfamiliar individuals?

Initiating a significant dialogue with someone unfamiliar could evoke initial discomfort and anxiety. Regardless of your level of expertise in initiating conversations or your difficulty with small talk, possessing the knowledge of how and where to commence is an invaluable skill.

Primarily, it is crucial to maintain an optimistic outlook when engaging in conversation, ensuring that a pleasant demeanor is expressed. Ensure that you exhibit appropriate posture and nonverbal cues, such as a genuine smile and open stance with arms uncrossed, to effectively express your happiness.

Inhale deeply: Prior to commencing the conversation, engage in a series of deliberate breaths. This intervention will facilitate a reduction in your heart rate and alleviate any feelings of anxiety.

Please monitor the stranger's availability closely: If the individual seems occupied or engrossed, aim to keep your conversation succinct.

11 Effective Methods for Initiating Conversations with Individuals You Do Not Know

1. Initiating a conversation with an unfamiliar individual can be facilitated by acquiring information through posing a question or a sequence of inquiries. In accordance with the prevailing situation, you may choose to inquire about the climatic conditions, their preferred lunch choice, or a common professional responsibility.

Take note of their response and deliberate upon additional inquiries or remarks that you could offer in order to sustain the flow of the conversation.

2. Express admiration to the unfamiliar individual

Offering a verbal commendation serves as an alternative approach to initiating a conversation with an unfamiliar individual. This approach generally leads to a constructive and amicable conversation regarding the item or element that has been admired.

3. Initiate a discussion on a widely-discussed subject.

Utilize the environment around you to initiate a discussion with an unfamiliar individual. For instance, in the context of an industry conference, you could engage in conversation with the person seated beside you during a session, inquiring about their thoughts regarding the event. If you are currently enjoying a meal, kindly direct the attention of the individual standing in front of you to your preferred culinary selection.

4. Describe yourself

An introduction is a straightforward method to initiate a conversation with an unfamiliar individual. This is particularly advantageous in situations where alternative discussion starters may not be readily evident.

It is highly probable that the individual you are about to be acquainted with will provide you with their name and relevant details concerning their role, thereby initiating a relaxed exchange of dialogue.

5. Inquire with open-ended questions.

Inquiring engaging questions serves as an additional effective approach in initiating a discourse with an unfamiliar individual. When one is attending a communal gathering and has the opportunity to inquire about the other individual's encounter, this approach proves to be most effective. Please contemplate the given circumstance: "I have never attended such an awe-inspiring workshop before." "What is your sentiment?"

In the majority of instances, the counterpart will engage by sharing their perspectives or recounting experiences from prior conferences they have attended, thus offering additional conversational material.

STRUCTURING THE CONTENT

You might have received valuable feedback concerning the duration of your communication, either before a corporate presentation or when drafting a company-wide email. The magnitude of the length holds significance, albeit not to the extent that one might assume.

One should consider their content as an offering on the menu of a thriving fast food establishment. The customer consistently expresses interest in learning about current trends or inquiring about the top three items. Subsequently, they express a desire to ascertain the location at which they can obtain further information. This supplementary information could comprise a selection of alternative items, such as 'vegan' or 'gluten-free', positioned just beneath the more widely sought-after, indulgent offerings.

Alternatively, it could be elegantly annotated as a footnote suggesting that patrons inquire about the daily special. This is what the fast food connoisseur desires, and you are obliged to accommodate their preferences.

In order to align the content in a manner that maximizes its usefulness to the recipient, it is imperative that we embrace the concept commonly referred to as the pyramid principle. It is alternatively referred to as the iceberg principle. Consider the geometric structure of a pyramid and divide it into three distinct tiers. Consider envisioning your conclusion as the tiniest stone positioned at the summit, being substantiated by a double layer of stones beneath it.

The underlying layer presents the indisputable evidence that ultimately substantiates the conclusion. The subsequent stratum pertains to the substantiation that bolsters the underlying suppositions. Certainly, it is possible to have multiple layers, but the emphasis is on maintaining a layered structure. This means that when explaining a certain layer, one should provide the evidence from the immediate layer below (referred to as direct evidence) without unnecessarily complicating the message with extraneous information that may hinder the intended goal of driving action. To facilitate ease of understanding, it is advised to familiarize oneself with the three layers commonly recognized within the industry.

In light of the evidence presented, it can be inferred that...

Conclusive evidence IN ADDITION TO corroborating pivotal statements

Corroborating evidence OR Empirical data OR Premises

It is crucial to bear in mind the objective of communication, which is to inspire individuals to take action.

In order to effectively incite action, it is imperative to commence by presenting your conclusion, followed by the development of supporting arguments or the provision of compelling evidence. Hence, it is referred to as the pyramid principle.

Barbara Minto, an esteemed graduate of Harvard Business School, is the renowned creator of the pyramid principle. She has authored a comprehensive book, available for purchase at a price of approximately $135, and offers an online course that delves into the intricacies of this invaluable methodology. The pyramid principle adopts a hierarchical perspective, as opposed to the conventional structure observed in scientific literature, wherein the introduction is followed by the methods, results, and concluding remarks. As a result, numerous individuals who employ the pyramid principle hold the perspective that it represents a novel concept.

It's not.

It can be observed that individuals typically acquire information solely when actively searching for it. If it is they who inquire as to the reason, they are more inclined to be attentive. And individuals frequently inquire as to the reason behind this. Simon Sinek, the acclaimed author of Start With Why, places great emphasis on the notion that prosperous companies or viable concepts have indeed unearthed their underlying purpose. As a consequence, the individuals employed within such organizations or those who patronize their products exhibit a profound alignment with this fundamental raison d'être. His primary objective is to stimulate consumer or audience motivation towards purchasing a product or adopting an idea; however, it is crucial to recognize that he also places significant emphasis on the manner in which the message is effectively conveyed.

Locating The Appropriate Ladies

So, you are prepared to engage in social interactions with women, correct? But where?

Where might one encounter a suitable woman who aligns with one's particular interests? And upon discovering her, how can one ascertain that it is worthwhile to engage with her?

Where Do I Look?

In all locations, one might assert...

Females are present in various spheres, and a corresponding chance to engage in conversation and engage in light-hearted banter with them exists. Certainly, while certain locations may offer a greater number of available positions compared to others, it is imperative to remain receptive to potential opportunities at all times. One might find themselves waiting for a bus, at a gymnasium, or merely traversing a thoroughfare. Should you come across an individual who piques your interest, an opportunity presents itself.

Nevertheless, there are certainly certain venues where one may encounter women and avail oneself of a more conducive environment for engaging in flirtatious interactions. I have reserved a designated section in the subsequent chapters to explore more challenging examples, in addition to the apparent ones. However, at this juncture, I present a selection where you may find some success.

Karaoke

No, please wait a moment, I am being sincere. Many individuals hold the belief that karaoke bars are considered trite, however, this perception can contribute to the enjoyment factor. It is a common tendency for individuals to occasionally engage in actions that may result in a less dignified perception of themselves. In the presence of alcohol, these tendencies are further amplified, fostering an environment that encourages individuals to relax, enjoy themselves, and relinquish their inhibitions.

I highly recommend refraining from serenading the bar with lengthy songs like "American Pie" or any other unless you possess professional singing skills. Maintain brevity and ensure an enjoyable tone.

Lounge and cocktail establishments within hotels

A significant number of individuals who engage in travel often experience feelings of solitude and eagerly embrace the opportunity to forge new acquaintances. A lounge presents a prime opportunity to engage with women, allowing for conversation and the refinement of one's burgeoning flirtatious abilities.

Frequently, female individuals who are present in a hotel bar and enjoying a beverage exhibit advanced age and possess extensive experience engaging in professional discourse. It is advisable to enhance your self-assurance as you are aware that your prospects for initiating a conversation and engaging in flirtation are more favorable.

Engaging in romantic or flirtatious interactions within a bar setting may present challenges. In a circumstance where you are encountering an unfamiliar individual amidst a cacophony, particularly amplified by music, it is of utmost importance to ascertain that you convey oneself in a favorable light, so as to avoid instilling any sense of unease or apprehension in your counterpart. However, one must ascertain the effective communication of their message even in situations necessitating the projection of every word. Would you kindly extend an offer to procure a beverage for them or suggest that they acquire one themselves? What guidelines should be followed when engaging in flirtatious behavior within a noisy setting? Several recommendations for effectively engaging in flirtatious behavior at a bar encompass:

Maintain a pleasant facial expression while establishing direct visual contact. This method is an uncomplicated approach that you may employ to demonstrate your interest, while refraining from verbal communication.

Approach an individual and initiate a dialogue. Perhaps inquire about their preferred sports team as a means of initiating conversation. Show your interest.

Kindly take a seat beside the individual and inadvertently make contact with their arm. This will inevitably capture their attention, consequently creating an opportunity for you to engage in conversation with them. Following that, you may express remorse for the accidental collision and extend an invitation to procure a beverage as a gesture of goodwill. This allows the individual to securely hold the beverage (given the prevailing need for caution in society) while simultaneously promoting further discourse.

Use humor. Despite limitations in terms of speaking volume or variations in vocal tone, humor can still be employed as a means of communication. Initiate interaction by sharing a light-hearted moment through the display of your dance moves or by recounting an amusing anecdote. The objective at hand is to put the other individual at ease and elicit laughter to be shared between both parties. In the event that their response lacks laughter, it is evident that their level of interest is negligible, thereby granting you the option to disengage from the interaction.

Kindly request their participation in a dance. This approach conveniently enables one to ascertain the level of interest someone has in them. In the event that they decline, it would be appropriate to redirect your efforts elsewhere.

Engaging in interpersonal expressions of interest and attraction within a social establishment such as a bar or a night club can present challenges, but by employing tenacity and innovative approaches, one can enhance the likelihood of achieving desired outcomes while minimizing personal discomfort.

CHAPTER 5

Comprehend your anxieties

Fear can serve a practical purpose as long as it does not completely incapacitate us from taking action. Fear serves as a constant reminder of our human nature, acting as a deterrent against recklessly stepping in front of moving vehicles, and triggering instinctive reactions like the "fight or flight" response, thereby enabling us to evade perilous circumstances. Nonetheless, in our role as communicators, it is imperative that we acknowledge any apprehensions that might hinder our ability to engage with others through verbal or written means.

Numerous individuals often refer to the insightful statement made by Franklin Delano Roosevelt, in which he mentions that the sole object of our apprehension should be fear itself. However, it is equally captivating to consider a more pragmatic viewpoint expressed by his spouse, Eleanor, who proclaimed, "Engage in a daily endeavor that invokes fear in you." The esteemed first lady argued that instead of allowing anxiety to hinder our progress, we should accept it and continue to forge ahead.

Even within the professional realm, apprehensions play a pivotal role, exerting a pervasive constraint on individuals.

This implies that an individual's level of education can be exceptionally high, yet they may lack substantial value to potential employers if they face challenges in effectively conveying their knowledge.

Extensive research in this field over the years has revealed three key qualities that employers universally seek, irrespective of the specific position they are hiring for. These qualities encompass effective verbal and written communication abilities, adept problem-solving skills, and the capacity to collaborate successfully with others.

Primarily, employers seek to ascertain a candidate's aptitude for effective communication, irrespective of the position they are poised to assume.

With that being stated, what, in your opinion, constitutes people's greatest apprehension? A multitude of surveys and interviews have indicated that the primary preoccupation among individuals is public speaking.

Nevertheless, there exists solely a single method to conquer the apprehension of asserting oneself and articulating one's thoughts: Take action!

Do you experience challenges in expressing your thoughts or emotions? Numerous individuals, regardless of whether they acknowledge it or not, harbor apprehension towards engaging in communication. There may be occasions wherein it proves challenging to disclose one's innermost emotions to another individual. Nevertheless, the less attention you pay to your apprehension in regards to communication, the more it will deteriorate.

Fear arises from the instinctive drive for personal safety or the inherent desire to cultivate a favorable perception from others. It may prove beneficial in specific circumstances, though commonly it poses an obstacle. Yielding to the trepidation of interpersonal interaction prevents individuals from effectively conveying their own truth, fostering genuine connections, and experiencing a rich and fulfilling existence.

Initially, the prospect of overcoming contact anxiety may evoke trepidation. However, with dedication to honing one's skills, the process can become more manageable. To achieve the utmost strength of your personal character, it is imperative to acquire the skill of having unrestricted and proficient communication with others.

Utilizing emotional intelligence to enhance your professional trajectory

The majority of our daily business decisions are predicated upon the influence of emotions. We hold the belief that choice A surpasses choice B. Consequently, our decision-making process often relies on our emotions or instinctual sentiments.

Individuals must cultivate self-awareness in order to enhance their lives and acquire a deeper understanding of their true selves. It pertains to comprehending the factors that drive their motivations, the sources of their fears, their areas of proficiency and vulnerability, and related aspects.

It is imperative for individuals to possess a thorough comprehension of their emotional state in the context of collaborative work. Individuals who possess congruent emotional perspectives are more predisposed to achieve and experience optimal growth.

In essence, conceptualize emotional intelligence as the act of empathetically stepping into another individual's perspective. It pertains to comprehending individuals' cognitive processes.

In light of the increasingly diverse teams and global nature of businesses, it is imperative to possess a heightened sensitivity toward the emotions and concerns of others. This is particularly crucial given the complexities involved in cross-cultural interactions and the varied ways in which emotions manifest themselves. The prevalence of differing personal criteria regarding the management of emotions could potentially present some additional complexities or challenges.

Emotional intelligence is essentially defined as the capacity to comprehensively comprehend, effectively articulate, and proficiently regulate one's own emotions. In addition, it encompasses the aptitude to cultivate and sustain healthy interpersonal connections, coupled with the capability to cogitate rationally in order to address challenges in high-stress situations. The ensuing exercise will aid in enhancing your comprehension and utilization of emotional intelligence.

Please recollect a recent occurrence that you deem to be anxiety-inducing and envision yourself as an observer rather than a participant, adopting a perspective as though you were gazing downward at this particular scenario. As you transition from the position of the participant to that of the observer, be cognizant of the accompanying transformation in your emotional condition. This newfound self-awareness, devoid of any emotional biases, will facilitate a lucid assessment of how this situation is affecting you and how you are influencing others.

This can assist in advancing your professional trajectory, as it will facilitate the more efficient management of your cognitive processes. Over time, one can observe the repercussions they have on others, facilitating the discernment of effective approaches when seeking to modify the beliefs or perspectives of others. Furthermore, it is of utmost significance to note that by acquiring a comprehensive comprehension of individuals' emotional states, you will effectively circumvent the substantial hazards that frequently arise from an inadequate grasp of such sentiments.

6. Exercising restraint in not articulating unexpressed ideas by others

Occasionally, we might find ourselves elucidating or articulating the ideas or sentences of our counterparts. This constitutes an extremely unfavorablebehavior. It diminishes the credibility of the speaker and alters the intended significance. Please pay full attention to the complete dialogue. Allow the speaker to finish their own sentences. Allow them to take a moment of reflection to determine if they require assistance in articulating their thoughts. Don't complete their sentences.

I have observed the extent to which this inclination can give rise to perplexity. It is highly probable that our comprehension of the matter is entirely mistaken. Our thoughts engage in various forms of diversion, often leading us astray into entirely unsuitable paths. This may give rise to unwarranted conflict.

Additionally, it is important to be mindful that expressing one's opinions prematurely, without a comprehensive grasp of the matter at hand, can result in divulging one's intentions too readily. There is a possibility that you could inadvertently extend a excessive offer.

7. Proper closure

Typically, in accordance with established protocols, complete closure of a communication would involve the subsequent elements:

Both the speaker and the listener are in agreement.

The task deliverables, anticipated outcomes, and subsequent actions have been clearly defined.

It is evident as to which individuals will undertake specific tasks.

The agreed-upon deadline has been established.

The parameters for evaluating the objective have been established.

Please ensure that the conversation is concluded appropriately. Reiterate the concluding elements prior to concluding the conversation/communication.

8. A Parting Joke

This anecdote brings to mind a humorous anecdote.

Friend: May I inquire about the key to the contentment in your marital union?

Lady: I engage in intellectually stimulating conversations with my spouse. We do not retire to slumber until we have attained sufficient resolution.

Friend: That is fabulous. May I inquire as to the reason for your apparent fatigue?

Madam: I implore you to dedicate a span of three days and nights in pursuit of achieving a satisfactory resolution...

6. Proper closure

Complete termination of the communication requires the following actions:

Verification of comprehension - The presenter ought to verify the comprehension of the matter under discussion with the recipient, in order to ascertain that both parties share a mutual understanding. An alternative approach would be to assign a listener with the task of providing a comprehensive summary of the discussion at its conclusion, for the collective advantage of all individuals in attendance. In the event that the summary is accurate, express gratitude to the recipient; otherwise, make any necessary additions, deletions, or clarifications.

Facilitating additional input/clarification – Ensure that there is a means of communication available for the audience to contact you. Kindly instruct them to reach out to you should they require any additional clarification or assistance. Alternatively, kindly provide your email address if you prefer. Additionally, it is important to allocate time for responding to the inquiries if you are approached.

CHAPTER 6

EMPATHY

T

The term empathy originates from the Ancient Greek word empatheia, which translates to "feeling into." Empathy encompasses the capacity to place oneself in the shoes of another individual and understand their subjective perceptions. Empathy arises within us when we perceive or discern the emotional state of another individual, and when we are able to assume their point of view, discerning and comprehending their emotions within a specific context.

There is a frequent tendency for individuals to conflate empathy and sympathy. Empathy can be defined as the capacity to comprehend and experience another individual's emotions, whereas sympathy encompasses the act of feeling sorrow or expressing compassion towards someone else. While one might have a sense of sympathy towards individuals affected by floods, it is only through personal encounter with a comparable situation can one truly develop genuine empathy towards them.

Acquiring empathy necessitates establishing a profound connection with our own emotional experiences and cultivating a sense of ease within the realm of emotions. Numerous individuals exhibit unease when it comes to the manifestation of emotions, specifically those that society tends to view negatively, such as grief, rage, envy, or apprehension. Frequently, the initial inclination when confronted with these emotions within ourselves or others is to steer clear of them.

In the personal development workshops that I facilitate, attendees have the opportunity to establish a profound rapport with their inner selves or establish a strong resonance with the individuals present in the vicinity, as we delve into inquiries surrounding significance, inclusion, and individual heritage. Tears are not uncommon. It is intriguing to witness the responses exhibited by fellow participants. A portion of the individuals maintain composure, with tears welling in their eyes, whereas others exhibit restlessness or promptly engage in passing around tissues. Attaining a considerable degree of self-awareness and embracing others' emotional experiences is essential to effectively maintain their emotional space. While it is only natural for us to seek solace in one another's presence, frequently our gestures of consolation, such as comforting pats on the shoulder or offering tissues, stem from our desire to alleviate our own unease and divert others from experiencing their own emotions. Individuals who possess a heightened level of self-awareness are capable of perceiving and understanding the emotions of others, exhibiting empathy, and providing support and understanding during emotional experiences.

What is the significance of this in the professional environment? As per the findings of the Harvard Business Review, empathy is described as a profound emotional intelligence that exhibits strong correlation with cultural competence. Empathy, as possessed by individuals, facilitates the ability to perceive the world from the vantage point of others and comprehend their distinct viewpoints." Empathy establishes interpersonal connections, fostering resonance and granting individuals the sensation of being acknowledged, listened to, and comprehended. When individuals perceive that their thoughts and emotions have been acknowledged and comprehended, they experience a sense of security and are more inclined to be open to alternative perspectives, participate in cooperative efforts to address challenges, and engage in ventures involving potential uncertainty. This cultivates an atmosphere of trust, which fosters the establishment of connections, fortifies interpersonal ties, and nurtures allegiance. Within this particular setting, individuals experience a sense of security in voicing their thoughts and viewpoints, thus facilitating an environment conducive to the flourishing, creativity, and prosperity of businesses.

LEADING THE ACTIVITY

Elucidate the concept of the "three c's" (confidence, clarity, and control) and furnish illustrations of how they can be employed in assertive communication.

Encourage the adolescents to formulate and subsequently examine different instances of assertive communication, specifically gauging the level of assertiveness (or passivity/aggressiveness) exhibited.

Present a small selection of chocolates to an individual adolescent. Grant the remaining adolescents a brief opportunity to persuade the individual who is in possession of the confectionery to relinquish it. Subsequently, employ assertive language to persuade the child in possession of the confections to continue to keep them.

Upon the conclusion of the designated period, instruct the adolescents to compile a succinct account detailing their sojourn at said location.

Allow the other children to share the responsibility of holding the candy and utilize their assertive communication abilities to maintain possession.

Discuss the diverse modes of interaction during the course of the exercise.

DISCUSSION QUESTIONS

•What were your thoughts and sentiments when someone attempted to seize the confections from your possession? Please provide an example in which you demonstrated assertive conduct.

• Provide an instance wherein the utilization of assertive language would have been more desirable compared to aggressive or passive language.

- What advantages can be gained from acquiring assertive communication skills?

PRO TIPS

- Facilitate a brief "pausing and assessing" session to realign the group in the event that a teenager is expressing irritability or aggression during the task.

- Following each segment lasting approximately one to two minutes, highlight one exceptional phrase or instance of powerful communication.

Apologizing Sincerely

Instilling in young individuals the value of offering genuine apologies.

Materials Required: Plastic Easter eggs containing coins (or an alternative item for teenagers to pass amongst themselves)

Timeframe: 10 to 15 minutes

Ideal for a group ranging from four to fourteen individuals.

LEADING THE ACTIVITY

Engage in a dialogue pertaining to the parameters of acceptable conduct while offering an apology. Place emphasis on notable instances of positive behavior, such as exemplifying honesty and avoiding the act of attributing blame to others.

Arrange the adolescents into dual rows, maintaining a distance of approximately three feet between them, while ensuring that the individuals in each row are positioned to face one another.

Distribute the eggs. Subsequently, instruct the groups to engage in a reciprocal exchange of the eggs. Whenever a teenager successfully catches an egg, they regress in their progress.

Request that the individual responsible for the mishap involving the egg extend a sincere and heartfelt apology.

If you perceive their apologies to be genuine, let the game recommence.

Ensure that both parties of the adolescent partnership apologize, particularly in situations where it is unclear who initiated the conflict.

In the event that you have doubts regarding the sincerity of an apology, it is advisable to propose a temporary separation between the involved individuals for further discussion.

Terminate the game if there remains a solitary pair or if the pairings exceed a distance of 10 feet.

Request that the individuals who were expelled from the game and are of younger age engage in a discussion regarding the genuineness of their apologies and explore potential avenues for improvement.

Effective Communication Tips

Effective Communication Tips

Phone/Voice mail/Text

1. Kindly ensure that your voicemail message prominently includes information regarding the anticipated timeframe for returning calls. This will alleviate the guesswork for the caller and effectively prevent them from making two or three additional phone calls.

2. Please adhere to discussing only one matter per voicemail. For more efficient addressing of multiple concerns, engaging in a synchronous conversation may be advisable.

3. Please assume a standing position while engaged in telephone conversations. A research conducted at the University of Southern California

found that the cognitive processing speed of the brain shows a notable increase ranging from 5% to 20% when an individual is in a standing position. Do you think it would appear somewhat absurd if you were to stand and perform your tasks? You will have the esteemed presence of Thomas Jefferson, Ernest Hemingway, and Winston Churchill, all of whom maintained an upright posture while engaged in their work.

4. Make written records during telephone conversations. Maintaining a record of information helps to keep your attention and active participation during the discussion.

5. Prior to concluding the discussion, it is advisable to summarize the points of agreement in order to prevent any possible misconceptions.

6. Please kindly refrain from sending text messages unless there exists a preexisting professional affiliation. Kindly seek authorization and transmit messages solely to those individuals who express consent to employ text messaging for professional correspondence.

7. Exhibit courtesy towards individuals' time. Please refrain from engaging in text messaging activities unless it is deemed necessary during official working hours.

Email

8. Employ the "subject" line for notification purposes, such as providing information about a changed meeting date (e.g., Meeting rescheduled to April 5), as opposed to solely identifying the subject matter (Meeting change). You

will enhance the likelihood of capturing individuals' attention.

9. It is advisable to exercise restraint in the frequency of employing the term "urgent", as excessive usage may lead to desensitization among individuals, causing them to overlook its intended significance.

10. Exercise caution when deciding what to include in your email, for one cannot ascertain to whom the message may be subsequently forwarded.

11. Please ensure that your email is succinct and focused. As a general guideline, it is advisable to ensure that emails do not exceed the length of a single screen.

12. It is advisable to refrain from employing sarcasm in your emails as it may cause confusion due to the inability

of recipients to interpret your intentions accurately.

13. It is advisable to abstain from sending an email while experiencing anger. Please compose the document, but refrain from transmitting it. Allocate a few moments to relax, subsequently review your email prior to initiating transmission.

Chapter 6:

The Key to Effective Communication Lies in Cultivating Confidence during Conversations

Confidence plays a pivotal role in the success of any individual engaging in conversation. It will prove challenging to persuade individuals to have faith in you when you lack self-assurance. Even with an array of strategies for success at your disposal, if lacking the requisite confidence to substantiate them, their efficacy will prove futile.

What is the Significance of Confidence?

The following elucidates the consequences that arise when one possesses an inadequacy of self-assurance in executing casual conversation, or any other task, for that matter, extending beyond mere social interactions:

1. Apprehension will invariably act as the hindrance to your progress.

If one is consistently governed by trepidation and apprehension regarding all potential adversities, there will be numerous endeavors left unattempted or unexplored. Fear of failure can often lead to inaction, causing individuals to forego opportunities and potential benefits, even those that may have positive long-term consequences. Engaging in a basic form of interaction such as approaching an individual and politely inquiring, "Greetings, may I inquire about your current well-being?" Can present difficulties in terms of effective management due to a heightened fear of experiencing embarrassment.

2. You will fail to seize potential opportunities.

This is particularly pertinent in a professional setting, where engaging in casual conversation presents a promising avenue for networking that may yield substantial advancements in one's professional trajectory. Foregoing and allowing them to elude you is closely associated with the aforementioned point, as that very same apprehension will impede you and instill hesitation when it comes to seizing the opportunities readily available to you. In one's existence, it has the potential to impede the establishment of fresh bonds, connections, and other important human interactions.

3. It will prove challenging for you to experience happiness.

Individuals who exhibit a deficiency in confidence typically experience a diminished sense of self-worth, perpetually preoccupied by their shortcomings, thereby impeding their ability to attain happiness. When one's thoughts are consumed by their perceived shortcomings, it becomes challenging to focus on the necessary steps towards self-improvement. Negativity possesses significant emotional potency, manifesting far more effortlessly than its counterpart, positivity.

Fogging

Addressing critiques and instances of sarcasm is an immensely vital aspect of cultivating assertiveness. In the event that you perceive a remark made by an individual to be hostile or designed to provoke you, you may employ the technique known as fogging. Fogging involves the act of obfuscating or diffusing acerbic remarks or disapproval, creating a figurative veil between the interlocutor and the individual initiating the conversation. Utilize the fogging technique as a means to enhance your assertiveness.

Attain a state of tranquility: It is through achieving a state of relaxation that you will acquire the capacity to effectively address criticism in a constructive manner. It is possible for you to experience feelings of tension and defensiveness when faced with criticism. This subsequently results in an instantaneous alteration in one's posture and body language, the modulation of their vocal tone, and a subsequent decrease in their capacity to deliver an efficacious response.

Do not engage in retaliatory behavior: By doing so, you shift the attention towards the other individual, thereby exacerbating the tension.

Restrain yourself: Typically, criticism is intended to provoke you or elicit a burst of emotion from you. The individual intends for you to become agitated by his comment. Therefore, it is advisable to restrict the individual from experiencing negative emotions altogether.

Emphasizing Safety: Occasionally, individuals who express criticism may resort to aggressive behavior. If one is cognizant of an individual exhibiting violent behavior, it is paramount to prioritize one's personal safety.

Perfection is not always obligatory: Should you find yourself unable to provide a fully potent negative critique, there is no cause for concern. There are instances when an ineffective piece of feedback holds substantial value.

Substantiate Perception: On certain occasions, it becomes distinctly apparent why an individual expresses themselves or responds to you in a particular manner. Please provide a justification for mitigating frustration, as well as ensuring that any response or retaliation is reasonable. The subsequent discourse will similarly be devoid of any negative aspects.

Take into account the Speaker's emotional state: Once aware of the other person's distress, ensure you express recognition of it. This affords the recipient a sense of gratification in feeling acknowledged and aids in their emotional restoration.

Acknowledge Constructive Feedback: Occasionally, embracing criticism can effectively diffuse any negativity associated with it. The primary objective of criticism is to emerge victorious in that particular scenario. By acknowledging or concurring, you establish a mutually beneficial scenario wherein the individual perceives a victory, all the while obscuring the entirety of the criticism. If one is aware of the correctness of the other party's perspective, it would be advisable to openly acknowledge it. This facilitates a candid exchange with the other individual.

Please be attentive: It is advisable to afford your critic the opportunity to express their viewpoint prior to offering a response. This facilitates the ability to be adequately prepared for an open and substantive discussion. By exercising active listening and exhibiting patience, the rate of the discourse will decelerate. Engaging in active listening does not indicate an acceptance or submission to criticism.

Inquire about particulars: When individuals employ sarcasm or criticism, they often exhibit an inclination towards ambiguity. Ensure that you inquire into the motives behind someone's criticism of you, exercising caution to maintain a respectful and restrained manner in your approach toward that individual. In the event that you encounter nonverbal or indirect criticism, it is imperative that you seek clarification by requesting further explanation. This will induce the individual to assume accountability for their statements and will also provide a compelling response to your inquiry for elucidation.

Do not Provide Justifications: When providing explanations, ensure clarity without resorting to offering excuses. Simply present the objective information and provide an elucidation of the sequence of events. Permit the other individual to possess their own viewpoints. Please refrain from attempting to alter their perspective.

Address the Critique's Tone: Your response should focus on the manner in which the individual expresses their criticism towards you. In the event that the individual has good intentions, it is imperative that one expresses gratitude for their candor. Alternatively, in the case of deliberate or malicious intentions, it is advisable to bring attention to the matter and recommend utilizing an alternative approach to convey their message. One must consistently possess the ability to discern between valid critique and undue criticism. When constructive criticism is imparted, it aids in realigning and rectifying matters. Nonetheless, in the event of an undue abundance, it could potentially impact one's confidence and self-worth.

Request for a pause: Should you desire to ponder upon the criticism prior to formulating a response, it is permissible to kindly request a brief intermission. This will facilitate introspection regarding the information conveyed to you, enabling you to craft the most favorable response.

It contributes to an increased lifespan.

I assure you, this is not a lighthearted statement. A comprehensive scientific study has revealed that individuals who possess a sense of purpose in their daily lives experience an extended lifespan. The researchers, namely Sone et al., discovered that individuals of Japanese origin, both males and females, who possessed a clear sense of purpose in life, commonly referred to as ikigai, exhibited a significantly longer lifespan compared to those who lacked a focused direction and simply moved aimlessly through their existence. 2008). This notion stems from the belief that having a sense of purpose enhances one's longevity by fortifying the body's resilience against stressors.

It is important to bear in mind that your purpose should extend beyond your vocation, as it is not solely confined to your career aspirations. I do not imply that you should neglect your professional pursuits; they undeniably hold significance. However, it is advisable not to solely dedicate your existence to this pursuit, as it may result in a significant portion of your time being consumed within the confines of a manmade structure, causing you to overlook the marvels that our world has to offer. I'm speaking from experience.

My occupation engulfed my entire existence. For an extended duration, I struggled to achieve a harmonious equilibrium between my professional obligations and personal life, inadvertently blurring the boundaries between them. I am confident that my previous deficiency in asserting myself played a pivotal role in necessitating additional hours spent working at the office. Coupled with my strong drive to excel, this easily diminished the pleasure derived from life. Please do not misunderstand me, it is indeed possible for you to achieve your career potential and lead a meaningful life; it is only necessary for you to discover the appropriate equilibrium.

As my confidence grew, it became increasingly uncomplicated to discern my purpose and synchronize my life in a manner that allows ample space for both industriousness and recreation, as the adage goes. I prioritized allocating time to attain certification as a first responder, which afforded me a sense of purpose beyond my professional endeavors. Moreover, it is due to this cause that I have developed a profound interest in exploring different places. A multitude of opportunities came my way once I mustered the bravery to advocate for my desires.

It facilitates the identification of essential elements.

Once you have a clear understanding of your life goals, you are able to distinguish between activities of significance and those that are futile. It is a common occurrence for individuals to have a multitude of responsibilities that inevitably leads to a consequential blurring of their priorities. Furthermore, when coupled with the pressures imposed by societal norms, it becomes increasingly challenging to maintain a clear perspective on the true essence of existence. Acquire a source of income, invest in a vehicle, enter into matrimony, purchase a property, embark on the journey of parenthood, engage in professional endeavors persistently, eventually cease work activities as retirement beckons. It appears as though we are presented with a set of instructions to adhere to, without taking into account the possibility that perhaps, a few of us have a preference for strawberry confetti cake rather than vanilla cake. And what about those who possess an affinity for chocolate? Is it truly the ultimate objective of your existence to concentrate on attaining financial stability, experiencing romantic love, and establishing a familial unit, or is there a deeper purpose that you may be overlooking? It is solely within your purview to provide an answer to that query. Nonetheless, from my perspective, there are additional factors at play. In light of this understanding, I refrain from expending efforts on endeavors devoid of significance in the broader context, and instead concentrate my attention on matters of genuine importance.

It serves as a source of motivation to propel oneself towards their true passion.

Upon embarking on my journey, I came to the profound realization that the world had a wealth of knowledge to impart upon me, far beyond what any textbook could ever provide. This inspired me to make proactive efforts in order to engage in more frequent travel. I remained enthused even during mundane days, as I was cognizant that with every passing moment, I drew nearer to the prospect of preparing my luggage and embarking upon an extraordinary journey. Furthermore, it is important to note that it is feasible to possess multiple objectives, or perhaps a main life purpose accompanied by subsidiary ones to enhance it.

I would not assert that traveling is the ultimate aim of my existence; nevertheless, it holds significance and could perhaps be better described as a passion. Regardless of the circumstances, dedicating oneself to a purpose provides a remarkable surge of vitality. The time has come when one no longer perseveres for the arrival of the weekend and abhors the onset of Mondays. If you find yourself presently trapped within that cycle, it is advisable to reassess your life trajectory. Do you have a genuine passion for your profession or does it serve as a means to achieve your desired outcome? In the event that your response aligns with the latter option, perhaps it is an opportune moment to embark upon the pursuit of an endeavor that carries significance for you. In order to proceed with this, it is necessary to firstly address a crucial query: "What is the essence of my existence?"

Without intending to dwell on the somber, it is an inescapable fact that all individuals will ultimately face mortality. Considering this information, do you have full certainty in your decision to allocate your limited time towards activities that do not ignite your spirit or contribute significance to your existence?

When one shuts their eyes at the end of the day, the passing hours and events become irrevocably consigned to the annals of history. It can be quite effortless to overlook the fleeting nature of our time when we become engrossed in the monotonous routine of everyday life. Monotony takes hold and we tend to overlook the profound wonder of existence. Nevertheless, upon discovering your life's purpose, you will embark upon a truly fulfilling existence.

Strategies For Mitigating Interpersonal Conflicts Within A Team

Conflict does not necessarily constitute an inherent element of Project Management. However, when confronted with a demanding situation, it is a probable outcome to have a team that comprises individuals from various backgrounds.

In the event that your team exhibits a high level of maturity and operates efficiently, it is possible that there may be no necessity for your intervention in order to effectively manage any conflicts that may arise among them. They might find a solution independently. However, in the event that you do encounter it, it is crucial to address it promptly, prior to its escalation.

Presented below are five strategies that can aid in effectively handling conflicts that may arise among team members.

One-to-one Chats

Arrange for a casual dialogue to take place with the main characters. Utilize this tool for the purpose of providing constructive critique and recommendations. If you are able to effectively communicate with individuals who hold differing opinions at an early stage, it is typically the sole intervention that will be necessary.

Elicit their dedication and devotion to the project.

Attribute any negative behavior to their enthusiasm.

Assist them in identifying a means to restore any harm inflicted upon their relationship.

Presenting it during a team meeting

Occasionally, the disagreement transcends the individuals directly involved. Subsequently, you may opt to address the matter in a public manner. However, should you choose to engage in conversation, it is advisable to maintain a focus on the matter at hand, avoiding personal attacks or criticism. Ensure that you adhere to the team's established ground rules that were mutually agreed upon during the inception of your project. It is imperative to maintain a constructive and meaningful dialogue.

Mediation

In more substantial conflicts, it may be necessary for you to assume a mediator's role in facilitating the resolution of the protagonists' dispute. Prior to the main discussion, it is imperative to personally acquaint oneself with each individual in order to gain a comprehensive understanding of their respective viewpoints. Subsequently, convene once more with each party to investigate opportunities for consensus and mending of relations. Ultimately, convene the main characters for the purpose of discussing and devising a mutually agreed upon course of action after a sufficient level of shared understanding has been reached.

What if one is unable to establish a shared understanding or agreement? Alternatively, what if they exhibit a refusal to engage in negotiations with one another?

Arbitration

Arbitration is the consequential progression from mediation. At present, you are no longer assisting them in locating their own means of resolving the issue. Conversely, you will preside over the issue and establish both a resolution and a path for progression. This approach will prove effective solely if one possesses the appropriate blend of authority and respect from both parties involved.

Confrontation

I have never had the need to engage in direct confrontations with team members, but it could be an option worth considering. Should you choose to undertake such action, it is imperative to acknowledge the tangible hazards involved.

So, prepare well. Ensure that you have comprehended all pertinent information and thoroughly evaluated your thoughts and the manner in which you intend to communicate them.

You also have the option of enlisting the participation of another team member. This could potentially serve the purpose of establishing an impartial observer or cultivating a support system for oneself.

Initially, direct the attention of the individuals central to the project towards its objective and purpose. Subsequently, utilize their sense of accountability and obligation to contextualize their reprehensible actions. As is customary, ensure that you can prevent the escalation of the conflict on a personal level. The focus lies on the actions exhibited, rather than on the individuals involved.

Reprimands and Discipline

Your final course of action is to admonish either one or both parties. It may be necessary for you to contemplate the possibility of excluding either one or both individuals from the project. These measures are of an extraordinary nature, therefore it is crucial to ensure that you execute them in a manner that is distinctly equitable, balanced, and in complete adherence to the policies and protocols of your organization. Take into account the possibility of receiving assistance from a sponsor or another esteemed colleague.

www.ingramcontent.com/pod-product-compliance
Lightning Source LLC
Chambersburg PA
CBHW052134110526
44591CB00012B/1721